Oscar and his Mouse

Written and illustrated by
Eleanor Fein

Hamish Hamilton
London

For Ishmael

HAMISH HAMILTON LTD

Published by the Penguin Group
27 Wrights Lane, London W8 5TZ, England
Viking Penguin Inc, 40 West 23rd Street, New York, New York 10010, U.S.A.
Penguin Books Australia Ltd, Ringwood, Victoria, Australia
Penguin Books Canada Ltd, 2801 John Street, Markham, Ontario, Canada L3R 1B4
Penguin Books (N.Z.) Ltd, 182-190 Wairau Road, Auckland 10, New Zealand

Penguin Books Ltd, Registered Offices: Harmondsworth, Middlesex, England

First published in Great Britain 1990 by
Hamish Hamilton Ltd

1 3 5 7 9 10 8 6 4 2

British Library Cataloguing in Publication Data
CIP data for this book is available from the British Library

ISBN 0-241-12782-3

Printed in Great Britain by
Cambus Litho Ltd
East Kilbride, Scotland

Oscar's mouse Maurice was his favourite toy. Oscar carried Maurice with him everywhere. He even took Maurice when he went fishing with his dad.

One day Mr Mog told Oscar that he had to go away on a long business trip. Mr Mog ran the Cat's Whiskers Catfood Company and was going to find more exotic recipes to put in his tins.

Oscar and his mum were very sad when Mr Mog went away. Oscar missed the trips down to the river and he missed sitting on Mr Mog's lap, listening to his deep, friendly purr.

Mr Mog sent home postcards from strange places. Each night as Mrs Mog tucked Oscar and Maurice into bed, they ticked off another day before Mr Mog would be home again.

Then, at last, the day arrived. Oscar
sat on the stairs with Maurice and waited
excitedly. They watched the front door.

When Oscar heard a taxi draw up and the
garden gate click, he knew it must be Mr
Mog. He jumped down the stairs.

"Dad's home! Dad's home!"

Mrs Mog ran to open the front door and
Oscar jumped into Mr Mog's outstretched
paws.

Mr Mog hugged Oscar and Mrs Mog and didn't forget to pat Maurice on the head. Oscar helped to carry in all the bags and Mr Mog sank into a deep armchair. Oscar climbed onto his lap with Maurice.

"It's so good to be home," purred Mr Mog. "I've missed you both so much."

Mr and Mrs Mog and Oscar all had a cup of warm cream while Mr Mog told them about the countries he had visited. Then Mr Mog, wiping the cream from his whiskers, got up and rummaged through his bags.

"I've brought you both a surprise," he said. He fished out a round box and handed it to Mrs Mog. "This is for you, my dear."

Mrs Mog lifted the lid. Inside was a magnificent new hat.

"Now Oscar, I wonder what I have for you!" Mr Mog reached into his bag and pulled out a large parcel. He gave it to Oscar.

Oscar settled Maurice on the floor
beside him and began to unwrap the
present.

There were so many layers of paper
to take off.

The mound of paper on the floor grew
higher and higher.

He tore off the last layer of paper and
there was a beautiful shiny red robot
mouse!

Mr Mog crouched on the floor beside
Oscar to show him how to work the
mouse. It had a separate control box.
Oscar pressed the buttons one by one. The
robot sprang into life. His lights flashed,
his ears swivelled and his arms waved.
Oscar pulled the small lever and the robot
went humming across the floor, letting out
little squeaks.

Oscar steered the mouse round the
chairs and under the table. He sent him
out into the hall and back into the room
again. He was so excited by his new toy
that he forgot all about his old friend
Maurice.

He played with the robot until it was
time for bed. Mrs Mog helped Oscar to
clear up all the wrapping paper, which
was scattered over the floor. They scooped
up heaps of paper and threw it into the
dustbin outside.

Oscar kissed Mr Mog and Mrs Mog goodnight and carefully carried his robot up the stairs to bed.

The robot took up rather a lot of room in the bed, but soon Oscar was fast asleep.

Oscar was woken early in the morning
by the dustmen emptying the dustbins
underneath his window.

When he climbed back into bed beside his robot, Oscar suddenly remembered Maurice. He thought very hard about where he had left him. He looked down his bed. Maurice wasn't there. He looked under his bed. Maurice wasn't there either. Oscar began to feel very worried.

He ran to Mr and Mrs Mog's bedroom.

"I've lost Maurice! I can't find him in my room!"

Mr and Mrs Mog put on their dressing gowns and came downstairs. They all searched for Maurice, but he was nowhere to be found.

Then Oscar suddenly remembered the dustbin full of wrapping paper.

He ran outside but, before he looked into the bin, he knew what he was going to find. He had watched the dustmen this morning and, of course, the bin was quite empty.

"We must have thrown Maurice away with the paper. Oh, I've lost him for ever!" Oscar began to cry.

Mr Mog took Oscar on to his knee.
"Don't cry Oscar," he said gently.

But Oscar couldn't help it. He was very
excited by his new robot mouse, but to
lose Maurice was terrible. He was a
special old friend and Oscar felt a big
gap without him. He was very sad.

Mrs Mog tried to cheer Oscar up.
"Let's get dressed, then we'll go down
the street to the market and buy a big fish
for lunch."

At the fish stall, Mr Paws the
fishmonger offered Oscar his favourite
kind of fish – a big herring. But even the
sight of his best meal didn't make Oscar
feel any happier. He could only think
about Maurice.

On the way home, they walked past a brand new dustcart which was parked in the street. The front of it was decorated with a collection of toy animals.

"Look at the front of that dustcart!" cried Mrs Mog.

But Oscar was only reminded even more of Maurice and couldn't bear to look. He covered his eyes with his paw.

But something had caught his eye. Oscar peeped out from behind his paw. There was a little figure sitting behind the windscreen and there was no mistaking it – it was Maurice!

Oscar ran up to the driver's window and banged on the door with his paw. The driver peered down.

"That's my mouse!" cried Oscar, pointing up at the windscreen.

"Well, I never!" said the dustcart driver. "That poor little thing was found in a bin. We had to rescue him. He looked so lonely." The driver winked at Oscar and handed down the precious mouse.

"Oh, thank you!" said Oscar, clutching Maurice and hugging him tight. "I thought I'd never see him again."

Oscar was so happy to have Maurice
back again that he had a smile on his face
all the way home.

Maurice was rather grubby after his
adventure in the dustbin, so Mrs Mog
wiped the marks off his face and washed
his clothes. When they had all eaten the
delicious herrings, Oscar played with
his toys. The new robot mouse was
introduced to Maurice and gave him
a ride all round the house.

That night in bed Oscar went to sleep
with his paw round both his mice. He was
even more squashed this time, but Oscar
didn't mind at all.